A Hopeful
Single Life

A Hopeful
Single Life

Z- 4

A HOPEFUL SINGLE LIFE

iUniverse books may be ordered through booksellers or by contacting:

iUniverse
1663 Liberty Drive
Bloomington, IN 47403
www.iuniverse.com
1-800-Authors (1-800-288-4677)

ISBN: 978-1-5320-0456-8 (sc)
ISBN: 978-1-5320-0457-5 (e)

Library of Congress Control Number: 2016912905

Print information available on the last page.

iUniverse rev. date: 08/05/2016

$\mathscr{C}$ontents

THERE IS STILL HOPE

THE STORM HAS PASSED

Acknowledgements

To my beloved Baptist Church where I was married and still being taught and encouraged today. I am shown love and respect which is inspiring for me and my family.

To my beloved grandparents and mother who raised me from childhood in a warm and Christian home. They loved me and showed their care in meaningful ways.

To my beloved children and grandchildren who remain by me always showing dedication and much love to me. Their lifestyles making me proud and thankful they are my loved ones.

Introduction

Lisa is a beautiful woman who had many experiences in life. She was loving and kind to people. Yet, because of her warmth in character, she was easy to become involved in various male relationships.

It was not that she was on the wild side on purpose, but she was looking for her "Soul Mate". Each man she dated was believed to be "the one" for her. She would end up broken hearted and alone for some disappointing reason.

It was after a life threatening incident in her marriage that put her on a different path. She decided to change her life and met someone "Special". The man of her dreams finally arrived in her life and took her away traveling.

Yet, he too went away in war for a few years to return to saying he was moving on without her. Lisa, being very upset but holding on to her sanity, began to turn the channels on her TV remote and found what would be just the key to her life all the time.

Enjoying Life

Chapter 1

What a Friend

The phone rang again as James stepped out of the shower. He walked calmly across the floor and picked up the phone as he said, "Good morning Lisa, why are you calling so early this morning?"

Lisa was shaking and nervous as she said, "James I have to get out of this religion. It is stressing me and I do not believe in it anymore. I want to go back to Christianity, which I was raised in all my childhood life."

As James sat down on his bed, he excitedly said, "Oh, Lisa this is great news. I have wanted this for you and now it is happening. What do you want me to do?"

Lisa hesitated, then she said, "James I want to visit you in Los Angeles to have you help me to get my mind together. I need a change in environment for about a week. James please help me!"

Silence lingered on the phone for about a minute until James said, "Lisa you know that I am your friend and I am here for you, but are you sure this is the change you want to make for long term?"

"James I have never been surer about anything. I just need your support to change my perception about the world." Lisa said with excitement in her voice.

James stood up and walked to his glass door and said, "Lisa, I will make the flight arrangements, but when can you arrive?"

"Well, I can leave this Friday and stay a week," Lisa said.

"Great! I will call you later with the itinerary"

"James, I love you!"

"I am here for you. Lisa you will have a wonderful time here in LA and begin your new phase in life. I love you too," replied James.

Chapter 2

My Time with Jed

Lisa began to twirl around her room happy as a bird. She took off her clothes and walked into her bathroom to take a warm shower. After her shower she turned on some soft music and lay on her bed, in her robe given to her by Jed. She held the robe close as she reminisced about her time with Jed.

Jed came walking through the salon door, with his eyes pierced on Lisa, as she smiles happily at him. He walked up to her as she sat under the hair dryer and said, "Baby, I have a gift for you, for your trip to Miami Monday."

Lisa raised the dryer hood to see him clearer. "Jed, did you say the gift is for me?"

"Yes, with one stipulation." Jed said as he placed the gift on the counter.

Lisa stood up and the other ladies looked at her with a surprise gaze knowing her hair was not dry after her brief setting under the dryer. Lisa smiling said, "Jed, I am still going to your father's church on Sunday. You know I want to show off and meet your daddy darling."

Jed looked astonished and said, "You must have read my mind that is exactly the stipulation for your gift. I will bring it to you when we have dinner tonight. By the way, where are we going this evening?"

"Darling, you surprise me because you seem to be good at it today," said Lisa.

"Ok I will decide on something quaint that will make you love me even more than your gift, if that is possible," said Jed.

"Well, let me get back under this dryer so I can look my best for this evening and the trip with your aunt, my wonderful hairstylist, who chose me to model in the hair show. I love the way you and your family loves me," Lisa said.

"Baby," Jed talking, "You are my lady and I will talk with you later Beautiful," as he gave her a kiss on the cheek and embraced her closely.

∞

As Lisa and Jed where exiting the church waiting to shake hands with Jed's father Rev. Robinson, Lisa liked in his eyes and spoke up with a smile saying, "It is a pleasure meeting you Rev. Robinson. I enjoyed your sermon on Jesus being the Way, the Truth, and the Light and no one comes to the Father except through him."

"Well" with a large grin, the pastor said, "You are as gorgeous as my son Jed mentioned to me and attentive as well. Perhaps you may come over for family dinner when you return from your trip to Miami."

Lisa bowed her head amazed that the Reverend knew about her hair show modeling trip and said, "Sir, I am honored that you are aware of the trip and I would love to have dinner with Jed's family," and she hugged Jed's arm even closer.

Rev Robinson, let go of their handshake and said, "Alright, it is a date. You just be safe and have a successful time."

"Thank you so much Sir and I am looking forward to visiting soon," replied Lisa.

Jed said, turning to Lisa, "Well sweetheart, glad you enjoyed the service and paid such close attention. My dad likes his messages to be remembered."

Lisa and Jed smiled at each other and walked to his Mercedes in the church parking lot.

≈

Chapter 3

Miami Beach Wonder!

It was a cool summer morning in New York as she walked on to her balcony and looked happily at the clouds. Lisa came out of her trend of thought long enough to dress and have some breakfast.

As she began to think, her thoughts led her back to the trip she shared with her hair stylist Sophie and the hair show in Miami.

≈

"Are you buckled in securely Lisa, while you're looking out that airplane window, saying goodbye to New York?" said Sophie.

"Yes, Sophie, actually wake me up once we arrive please. I can hardly wait to visit the Fountain Bleu Hotel," said Lisa.

"Yes, and do not forget the beach with the ocean waves," said Sophie.

Two days went by with Lisa and Sophie were seeing Miami Beach together with business associate

It was now Wednesday, the first day of the exhibition and contests. Lisa decided to venture out in the lobby by herself to do some sightseeing. The people were friendly and everything was made of brass as well as classy. The pictures of the historic celebrities on the wall made Lisa know she was in the most fabulous of hotel locations.

Suddenly their eyes met as she was walking down the stairs and he was coming up. Never had she seen such thick and dark hair, glowing tanned skin and clear eyes uniquely shaped. Lisa almost tripped but he laughed and caught her so calmly.

"May I help you?" He asked.

Lisa was so excited to be in his warm embrace, she unexpectedly said, "Yes, do you have any free time to show me around? I'm from New York," taking advantage of the golden opportunity.

He looked at her rather surprised and then he said, "I do have 1 hour so let us take a walk along the beach."

Lisa could hardly stand from shock with reply to her. This handsome, exceptional looking man was holding her by the waist walking her toward the bungalows of Miami Beach when suddenly Lisa came to herself.

≈

Lisa had been thinking about this trip all week and now she sitting on the plane headed for Los Angeles. The stewardess had said to buckle up to prepare for the airplanes decent into the city.

"So you made it here alright I see," said James.

"Well the turbulence was a bit disturbing at times," said Lisa.

"Yes, I know what you mean," said James. "But you are here now, let's go get dinner and relax."

As Lisa sat in the park in New York, thinking of her LA visit with James, she thought of the beautiful restaurants that they had visited which had such rich appeal. The cars of all styles imaginable are in Los Angeles. And that in depth conversations she had with James was astounding.

Mainly the decision made was that Lisa would apply to Syracuse University for Art. Just the thought led her to stand up from the park bench and start home to get the process underway. She was so excited and determined to make their plans come true.

"Well Lisa, welcome to SU and your portfolio is exceptional as everything seems to be in order," said the admissions professor.

"Oh, I'm so excited to attend here," said Lisa, with a large smile on her face.

∞

It had been several weeks now that Lisa had been attending college classes. The atmosphere of the college was motivating and very informative. She had met several new friends and had two study partners.

Yet, in her Art 101 classes there seems to be an attraction between her and the assistant professor. H gave her a lot of attention and compliments on her work.

"Sure, I would enjoy coming to your Fashion Show this Saturday at the famous Syracuse Hotel," said assistant professor Sage.

"Oh, I am so excited," said Lisa. "The Fashion Show also includes dinner and dance after."

"Well, I will decide how long I will stay," said Sage.

"Fair enough," said Lisa.

Sage and Lisa were dancing and having a fantastic time. Then Sage said, "I'm ready to call it a night. May I take you home?"

"Sure" said Lisa and they were on their way to Lisa's home.

Once they arrived at Lisa's and had said their goodnight, Lisa reached over and kissed the professor seductively. He responded by embracing her face tenderly and things progressed to where they were in bed within a matter of minutes.

The next day after class the professor Sage said, "Lisa, I immensely enjoyed my evening with you but you know this cannot continue."

Lisa bowed her head, then looked up at him suddenly saying, "I know, I did not expect our relationship to continue but it was a wonderful experience."

Growing Power

Chapter 4

Meeting Franco the Super

As Lisa and Joy were entering the apartment building, a male voice said, "Hello Miss Lady, I know you are new in the building and I want you to know if you ever need anything, anything at all, just let me know."

Lisa looked at him straight in the eyes and said, "Are you talking to me Sir?"

"For sure dear," he said. This was the Superintendent of the building with a sly grin.

"Oh, I know how to call the office for my requests. Thank you anyways," said Lisa.

"Anything you say Ma am," he replied.

When Lisa and Joy entered the elevator Joy said, "I think he was coming on to you Lisa."

"I think so as well Joy," said Lisa.

"He is kind of cute and he has a nice set of shoulders."

They laughed and exited the elevator to enter Lisa's apartment. The ladies were preparing for what was to become their occasional neighborhood walks. Living t the apartment complex was warm and when seeing

Franco—the Super—was kept professional for several months, until one day there was an evening knock on Lisa's door.

"Who is it?" Lisa said.

"It is Franco" he said.

"How may I help you. I have not requested anything," She said, without opening her door.

"Actually I am here on a personal matter," he said.

Lisa hesitated for about a minute, then reluctantly opened the door just enough for him to come into view. "Yes, Sir how may I help you today?" Lisa said to Franco.

"Well, I been holding myself back, but I decided to ask you today, do you have a man?"

"Listen you have no business!" Lisa said with anger.

"Hold it a minute sweetheart. You are to me the most beautiful women in this complex and I been thinking about you. And I want to be here for you and that's all. I mean I would love to take you out an even go to church with you. I see you go to church."

"Oh, so you been stalking me?' said Lisa.

"Dear one, I work here and I see everything. It is my job to know what is going on here." said Franco.

"I just wanted to step up and be honest with you about how I feel, that is why I came to talk with you this evening. I am not trying to be shady but I am being honest with you. You are beautiful and I really want to get to know you better."

Lisa hesitated then said, "Listen Franco, you seem like a nice person, but let me think about what you have said and I will get back with you soon."

Franco smiles and bowed his head to her and happily walks away. Lisa closes her door and leans against it and said to herself, "What the hell is going on with this picture?"

Chapter 5

Should I or Should I Not?

In the weeks to come Lisa and Franco dated. Franco even attended church with her a couple times when he was off work. He bought her new clothes and gave her money just for her pocket he would say.

Then the night arrived after their walk in the neighborhood museum fountain area when they came back to Lisa's apartment. Franco began to put his advances on Lisa for more from her than usual. Lisa being taken with all his charms gave in and they began to make love. Everything was going well, until all of a sudden, Franco put his hand in a choking move on Lisa's throat. She became so alarmed that she pushed him off her, got dressed and went down the elevator to use her phone to call the police on the first floor lobby.

The police arrived and told Franco he had to leave. Franco was astonished and said, "Girl, after all I done for you and I'm treated like this. Give me back my money!"

Lisa went into her drawer and gave him the rest of his money as he was escorted away by the police.

A week went by with no conversation between Franco and Lisa even when they seen each other in their apartment complex area. Yet, one Friday evening as Lisa and Joy were going for their exercise walk, Franco and another man approached them.

"Hello Lisa, this is my brother Justin and he is from New York City. He came here to help you understand that I in no way wanted to harm you. You mean so much to me," Franco started.

Suddenly Justin spoke up, "Lisa, I came here to support my brother in convincing you to come to NYC to meet our mother. She really wants to meet you after all the wonderful things Franco told her extensively about you."

Lisa looked at her girlfriend Joy as if she could not believe what Justin was revealing to her. All of a sudden Lisa said, "Joy will you come to NYC with me?"

Joy looked at Lisa as if she was out of her mind. Justin picked up on Joy's response and quickly said, "I'll pay for your hotel room and meals for the weekend."

Joy deciding this could be a brief vacation opportunity said, "What about entertainment?"

Franco stepped up and said, "Of course, we will go to a movie and club if you ladies like."

Lisa having a flash back of the incident when they were in bed together said abruptly, "No we can't go, I'm busy for the next few weeks with work."

Justin and Franco looked at each other then Justin 'd, "Look" as he reached into his pocket and pulled out his business card. He calmly extended it towards Lisa and said, "You give what we have shared with you some consideration and give me a call either way. Would you please?"

"I am very concerned about you two. You had a great relationship going which could grow into something more, I believe. And on that note I have to get back to my lovely wife." Justin moved towards Joy and said, "It was wonderful meeting you and I hope to see you again soon."

Franco looked at Lisa with eyes of sadness and he said, "Just give me the opportunity to show you that I may have been a little too kinky when I made love to you but it was all about having fun darling. I would apologize a thousand and one times if it would allow you to know I'm sincere."

Lisa lowered her head and turned her head to the left ever so slightly and took Justin's business card, putting it in her sweatpants pocket without reading it. Then Lisa said, "I've heard enough for now, we have to get going, goodbye gentlemen," as she began quickly walking away with Joy.

Chapter 6

Yes, I Should

"Oh, my goodness Joy I can hardly believe we are on our way to New York City'" said Lisa.

Joy turned her head looking out of the small plane window. Joy was not saying a word in response to Lisa. Then Lisa noticing Joy's silence said, "I know you think that I am wrong for giving Franco a second chance but I have come to love him and maybe he was just being to kinky when we were making love. I may have over reacted to his way of making love. Actually, since it was our first time."

Joy relaxed in her seat and not being convinced said, "Well, time will tell but at least we are getting a free two day vacation out of it in the Big Apple."

Friday evening they walked through the posh door of the fancy restaurant and were promptly seated at their large table in the corner. While waiting on their order being placed, they were having small chatter.

Justin and Franco's mother all of a sudden said, "Ladies you remind me of celebrities with your long weaved hair, beautiful manicured nails and wonderful body shapes. Do you exercise at a gym regularly?"

Lisa embarrassed and a bit annoyed about the "weave" statement cautiously and tactfully said, "Ms. Taylor, we walk in our neighborhood 2-3 times a week when the weather allows us. I am sure you are aware of the changes of the weather in upstate New York where we live since your son works in the area."

Ms. Taylor happily said, "So you walk...hesitating... in the neighborhood...isn't that a little frugal?'

Heat rose in the nostrils of Lisa and Joy this time but Joy spoke up saying, "Yes, it is frugal but beneficial and we do attend a gym during the colder months, which is expensive."

Joy wanting to say "Thank you so much" Yet, she smiled and looked at Lisa knowing that she made a point to the irritating mother.

Franco then said, "Listen ladies you are all beautiful and I'm very proud of how you all look—no matter what your beauty secrets may be."

Just then the terrific food was arriving to their table as Justin said, "Let us eat up!"

The atmosphere became much more pleasant and everyone seemed to enjoy themselves for the rest of the entire evening.

Chapter 7

The Engagement

(Buzz Buzz-phone ringing)

"Hello" said Lisa, as she answered her cell phone

"Hey girl, are you ready to go walking?" said Joy on her phone.

"Oh my goodness, I forgot to call you because Franco invited me to go see the movie," Lisa said with excitement in her voice. "Son of God! Would you like to come?"

Joy thought before saying, "Are you kidding me? You are going to learn about giving him a second chance."

"The trip helped me have more assurance that I must have jumped to the wrong conclusion about him," said Lisa. "Joy please just try to be understanding about our relationship because I do want to be with him."

"So since I do want you as my best friend as well," said Joy quickly "You are not getting rid of me because you are going to need me when the chips fall where they may," she laughed.

"Ok great!" said Lisa. "I'll call you tomorrow about the movie and my date. Bye!"

Weeks went by as Lisa and Franco grew closer and even went to church together on more occasions. There were no arguments, just fun and business activities. Lisa called Franco to request he meet her family for dinner on Sunday. They all seemed to mesh quite well.

Later in the evening Franco said, "Lisa, look under your pillow." Lisa pulled the sheets to cover her naked body as they lay in her bed together. Lisa sat up, raised the yellow satin pillow and she could hardly believe what she saw. She rubbed her eyes and reached for the shining silver object in the small black box.

She caressed it, rubbed it across her lips and then slipped it on her left ring finger. Then suddenly took it off and said, "You have to get on one knee and propose to me, Baby. We are not skipping that important traditional part."

Franco laughed saying, "You are my lady: sticking to the rules."

Then he pulled back the sheets and jumped happily out of the bed nude, reached for the ring from Lisa and walked over to her side of the bed. She was sitting there with this huge smile on her face as her legs dangling on the side of the bed.

Franco kneeled on one knee, with his genitals hanging between his legs. He took the ring, ever so delicately from Lisa's hand, looked her in the eyes, while holding her left hand and started saying, "Lisa, you are my Beauty and I want to help you experienc all the joy that life has to offer." And he stopped talking and slid the shinning diamond ring on her finger gently and said, "Will you do me the honor by becoming my first and only wife?"

Lisa bowed her head and began to cry. Franco reached for her and he said, "Darling what's the matter?"

Lisa took the sheet to wipe her eyes and said, "Sugar these are tears of joy. I was actually right to believe in you after all said Lisa.

"Baby I do not want to make you feel any other way," said Franco.

They kissed a lingering kiss and continued with their sultry steamy evening.

Chapter 8

The Marriage Arrival

Lisa's phone was ringing more today than any other day. She had tried to keep the news of her wedding to a bear minimum people. A few close family and friends. Yet, it seemed the news had reached more people than she expected. Now she was especially happy that her plans were to only have a church wedding with no reception and go directly on their honeymoon after the ceremony. Lisa was excited about this because their wedding was about their love for each other and not a show to pay forever.

"Franco my precious husband where are we going?" said Lisa as their limo pulled up to the airport front door after their brief but intimate service. The driver opened the limo door as they calmly stepped out to retrieve their luggage and head for the airport boarding routine.

Franco looked at Lisa with his eyes showing the joy of his surprise honeymoon and said, "We are going to Paris, the city of love."

Lisa could hardly speak and began kissing him on his lips hysterically until he had to hold her to calm her down.

Hours later as they lay in the large bed looking around the majestic room suddenly Lisa said, "How long are we going to be here."

"Well," said Franco, "our wedding was on Saturday, we are here in Paris today and I have to be at work by Wednesday."

"Oh, great Franco because I took a week vacation from work," said Lisa as they snuggled in the plush king size bed while drinking expensive wine.

"Excuse me but dinner will be served shortly so may I get you a certain drink?" said the flight attendant to the new Mr. and Mrs. Taylor as they looked up at her from their coach airplane seats.

They gave the flight attendant their drink desires and as Lisa looked out of the airplane window she said, "Darling, our visit here was spectacular even though we stayed in bed at the hotel the entire time.

Franco looked at her with a cunning gesture and said, "#1. I could not get enough of you. #2. You and I was all that mattered.#3. It was my strategy to leave you wanting more so that you would agree to come back here someday in our beautiful future as man and wife."

Lisa laughed happily and said, "I can see I am in for a ride with you my husband. And I look forward to it! have been wanting this for a long time and now it is ppening. Praise the Lord it is coming true!"

Chapter 9

Thriller Now

Hours went into days, days went into weeks, weeks went into years and Franco was being the man he wanted to line up for his bride. His bride was being what she expected a wife should be although her cooking was occasional and ordering out was usual. Otherwise, the sex was often and sensual. They had decided not to have children as they were in the process of developing their careers to a higher level with more money and opportunity. Yet, they did travel on short vacations within the continental United States while still attending church.

It was 3am in the morning and Lisa was pacing their apartment living room floor. The television was on but the sound was turned to mute. "Where could he be?"

The thoughts kept racing in Lisa's mind. She left messages for Franco on his voicemail. She wanted to call the hospitals but decided to wait until morning since she had not a call about him.

She sat down in the soft leather recliner in the living room to rest but quickly fell asleep. It was Tuesday morning and she suddenly awoke hearing the front door opening harshly. Lisa stood at attention and looked to see that it was Franco walking in the door with blood shot red eyes, clothes looking ruffled and him trying to turn his head from her gaze. "Oh Baby, I'm so glad your alright! You are alright aren't you?" said Lisa.

"Look Lisa before you start in on me, let me take a shower and lay down in bed, can you do that?" he said rather demanding. Lisa readily complied since he was now safe at home.

As Franco climbed into bed slowly and cautiously, being sure not to touch Lisa, who was already awaiting him on her side of the bed. He started to say something and then he stopped. Lisa taking it as a clue that it may be best for them both to sleep and talk later.

"Oh, stop Franco stop!" shouted Lisa as he punched her on the left side of her jaw then backslapped her on the right side of her jaw, followed by another blow to the left side of her jaw, until he felt her passing out.

He began to shake her for a minute, holding her by the shoulders until she regained consciousness. He dragged her into the living room and laid her on the sofa which he had bought her as a surprise birthday gift for her.

As she was coming to the point of speaking Lisa mumbled, "Franco, why are you doing this to me? I have done nothing wrong to you." He reached into his pocket and pulled out a small 22 caliber pistol he had borrowed from one of his boys and sat in the recliner Lisa had sat in earlier.

Franco pointed it at her and said, "I heard you were supposed to be leaving me," he started. "LEAVING ME!" he yelled louder. "After all the love and care I have shown you, you're going to leave me? Listen, I will shoot you in your heart and watch you die! I will then shoot myself in my head and join you! Leave me! Leave me!"

Lisa rose up a little to get her grasp of what she was hearing was true. Then she said, "Franco, I am so in love with you. I never said I was going to leave you. I never told anyone I was going to leave you. Please believe me darling!"

Abruptly, Franco stood up tore off his pajama shirt and stuck out his arm towards Lisa saying, "Lisa, do you see the tracks in my arm? They are there because of you. I was told you were leaving me and I tried to over dose rather than hurt you or be hurt by you. And I did not even die at all!"

Franco kept yelling and saying threatening accusations to Lisa. She was fearful and prayed someone would call her on the cell phone. Then there was a hard knock on their front door. Franco harshly said. "Who is it?"

"It's the police! Open the door right now!" said the officer demanding.

Franco's eyes became large and looked at Lisa's swollen face and bloody lips. He thought what should

I do? The evil inside him said, "What the hell? Deal with it." Franco had hid the gun in the recliner and he walked to the door and opened the door slowly.

"We received a report of a disturbance going on at this location," said the tall and confident police officer.

Franco, still feeling the effects of his evil actions on Lisa earlier, lifted his head standing boldly and said, "My wife is going to leave me and I cannot live without her! I love her! I done everything I can for her!" said Franco fearfully.

"Sir, where is she? Let us see her right now!" said the officer as his hand moved to his gun holster. The officer stood in the doorway of the apartment

"Here I am officer," said Lisa so relieved that her prayer had been answered. As the officer laid eyes on Lisa's abused face, torn down and painful look in her eyes, he shouted "Sir, you are under arrest!" and turned Franco around to hand cuff him harshly.

The other officer came in to assist in reading him his rights and lead him out. Then Franco began yelling to Lisa, "I really do not want to live without you! I have no life without you!"

Lisa yelled back with anger, "You should not have listened to your 'boys'." She calmly closed the door and rushed to call Joy after cleaning herself up.

Chapter 10

Rehabilitation

Lisa walked into the bathroom to see the damage done to her normally beautiful face.

"Oh my God" she cried while rushing to the phone book and could hardly turn the pages to find Vera House, a well known women's shelter for abused women.

"How long are you going to stay at the shelter?" Joy asked Lisa sadly.

"I guess until my face heals up. I do not want anyone to see me" said Lisa.

"My supervisor is making arrangements for me to be out of work for a while. He is going to let me keep my job because he values my work. And Joy do not dare say I told you so!"

Joy jumping up while still holding the phone saying, "Lisa we all have to learn one way or another. I am just glad that infidel did not kill you. Thank God you are going to be fine."

"Oh yes, Joy. I am finding me a new apartment I am never going back there where we lived. I a buying new clothes and new furniture when I leave this shelter" said Lisa.

"I do not want him to have any idea where I live. Also, I am getting an order of protection through the courts as well as a divorce as soon as possible. I will talk with you tomorrow. Thanks for being a good friend," as she walks into the library of the women's private location.

There is
still Hope

Chapter 11

The New Beginning

"Oh, I love your new place" said Leah "We can really enjoy this view."

"It is rather quiet here and the elevator works," said Lisa and they both laughed at that statement.

Later that evening Lisa decided to go sit in the lobby of her building and watch television. The people coming and going took away the boring feeling that she was having in her apartment. A magazine called her attention and as she was reading an article in it until she heard a voice say, "Excuse me, but could you tell me where the ATM is located in this building?"

It felt like slow motion as Lisa slowly looked up into the face that was so enchanting, in an army uniform and with a smile of pure gold. Lisa could not speak for a moment. Was she dreaming? She had been put on medication after the incident with Franco and she decided to see a psychiatrist to help her through all the issues of the changes in her life. Yet as she hesitated, the time slowly passed and that face, the unbelievable face was still there.

Lisa began to come into reality and said, "Would you like me...to tell you...where the ATM machine is?"

"Yes Ma'am, if you do not mind."

Lisa could now hardly contain her emotions. He was actually talking to her. But the only problem was: she did not know the answer to his question. How was she going to answer him?

She thought for a second and said, "It was so nice of you to ask me, but I am new to this building and I am not aware of there being an ATM at this location."

"Well, thanks anyways. I will just ask the office in the morning. You have a nice evening now," said the wonderful voice as it went away.

Lisa laid down the magazine and reviewed in her mind what had just occurred. Oh, what a special person. And out off all the people in the area, he came to Lisa to ask the question.

As Lisa stepped off the elevator going to her apartment, whom did she see taking out his garbage? It was him, the voice; the army uniform; the face.

He looked at her and smiled saying, "So I see you again?"

"Yes" Lisa said surprised.

"I actually live on this floor...apt c605." said the voice.

"You're kidding! I live on this floor, d600." said Lisa becoming a bit more cautious saying, "At least we are in separate wings of this apartment building."

"Hello, I am Uri," the voice introduced as he stretched out his hand towards Lisa.

With the quick and excited thought of being able to touch him, she smiled and reached out her hand towards him saying, "Hello, I am Lisa and I'm happily divorced."

He laughed and said "I'm happily never married." They gazed at each other for a lingering minute and suddenly stop laughing.

Lisa reluctantly said, "Well, I have to finish the rest of my day. Hope to see you again soon."

And he responded, "okay, for sure". Then they turned and went their opposite directions.

Chapter 12

Was That Joseph?

It was Wednesday afternoon around 6pm when Lisa decided to take a walk down the hall of her apartment to the rest area and watch the rain through the windows of the hallway. As she peered through the heavy rain drops hitting the windows she noticed a white Seville go pass on the street. It looked like a past memory.

Could it be Joseph? She started to breathe deeply and decided to sit in a nearby leather chair. She clutched the sides of her face with her hands with racing thoughts going through her mind; the thoughts going back to the scene where she first met Joseph.

They were at a nightclub and Lisa was setting at the corner of the bar with a girlfriend sipping rum and coke drink. Joseph spotted her upon his entrance into the club and had monitored her for a while before deciding to make his approach to speak with her. He was going to try to convince her to dance with him and if she did, only then would he buy her a drink, he thought in his mind.

"Well, I really enjoyed my evening with you Joseph," said Lisa as they stood outside the night club getting ready to depart to go home.

Joseph spoke up, "Listen, you are so beautiful. If you are not with anyone could you give me your digits?"

Lisa smiled and looked into his appealing eyes and said, "Give me your number and I will call you."

"When will you call me?" asked Joseph.

"Right now silly," said Lisa as they laughed.

$\mathscr{C}$hapter 13

Experiencing Memories

Joseph and Lisa met on occasions for tender and intimate moments. He worked the night shift so he would see Lisa whenever he could fit her into his busy schedule. Lisa accepted this situation even though she wanted a real relationship with Joseph. Yet, something with him was better than nothing so she kept up with the heartbreaking relationship.

Lisa leaned her head back in the chair as she continued to think about the past days with Joseph.

$\approx$

"Hello Joseph, we have to meet as soon as possible today," said Lisa on her computer to him.

He typed on his computer, "I will be right over after work early in the morning."

The next day, he walked through the halls to Lisa's door. "What's up?" said Joseph.

Lisa began to talk after pacing the floor. "Joseph I am pregnant. You know we been dating each other for

3 years off and on. I have to tell you that I tried a new birth control." He lowered his head and sat on the soft sofa as he was quiet.

Lisa said "Well, say something Joseph please. It did not work!" He still did not say anything but kept looking bewildered.

Then Lisa spoke up and said "Joseph, you know I am on medication because of my mental issues because of being Bipolar. And the medication could affect the baby's development and health. I do not want a deformed child. It would not be fair to the child or to us."

Then Joseph raised his head and said, "You must be kidding me! Then there is only one thing you can do." He walked over to her and held her agitated in his arms. They knew the only answer was for them to have an abortion.

Tears began to run down Lisa's face as she came to herself now looking at the rain. Just the thought of the entire process of getting that procedure in the New York City Clinic and staying overnight in a hotel made seeing the white Seville go by now such a dismal occurrence.

It was getting late so Lisa hurried down the hall to her apartment. She decided to watch a movie when the phone call from Nia rang. "Lisa, how would you like to visit my church with me and we go out for dinner after the service." said Nia.

Lisa abruptly said "Sure, I would love that actually."

They continued to talk as Lisa began to prepare what she would wear on Sunday. She knew that her faith in Jesus Christ had allowed her forgiveness of her sins and each time she went to church it seemed to support that circumstance.

Chapter 14

Uri Is For Me

Suddenly there was a knock at Lisa's door. It was getting late so she cautiously went to the door and looked through her door peep hole. It was Uri. She ran to the bathroom to groom herself quickly and raced back to answer the door.

"Hello Uri and how may I help you this evening?" Lisa happily said as she opened the door.

"Well Lisa I have been called to deploy in the war. I have to leave in 3 weeks" said Uri.

"You have to leave me?" said Lisa sadly.

Uri looked at her startled by her saying "leave me."

"Lisa, I've been waiting to ask you to dinner and a movie, are you able to come with me?"

"Definitely, Uri, when would you like to go?" said Lisa

"Next Saturday would be best for me" said Uri.

"Well, it's a date" Lisa answered with a smile.

Uri reached for Lisa and held her close in his arms. Oh, how she enjoyed the smell of his cologne and the tenderness of his embrace. He held her as if he did not want to let her go. She held him as if he was all that mattered at that time to her.

The next afternoon as Lisa was looking out her window she saw the black jeep of Uri pull in the parking lot and a woman got out with him. Lisa could tell by her appearance that she was hardly a relative. But, since she had no formal commitment with Uri, she could hardly make a scene about his new encounter.

So all evening Lisa's thoughts were racing about what they could be doing. The jeep never left after several hours. This made Lisa more and more jealous knowing now that intimacy was probably on their agenda. More and more thoughts of their meeting was flooding Lisa's mind until she finally fell asleep.

When she awoke the next morning and prepared for work, she decided to put them out of her mind. So, as she hurried to the elevator to drive to work. Yet, who was already standing there but Uri and his female conquest.

They all looked at each other because of maturity, they each said "Good morning." Uri smiled with an innocent look on his face and Lisa could hardly contain herself.

The elevator door opened and suddenly Lisa said, "You guys go ahead, I forgot something."

Uri looked at Lisa in the eyes knowing this was a gesture of jealousy and said, "You take care now." His words were a message in many ways.

Uri was gone more than a week. Lisa was upset, worried missing and wanting him so much. As Lisa was having a cup of coffee and dive into her latest book after her shower, her phone rang. As she reads the phone caller ID: it is Uri. She could hardly believe her eyes. She did not know whether to be happy or mad. But she calmly answered the phone being careful not to over react about what she had saw the last time she was in his presence at the elevator with his lady friend. Yet, being so thankful that he was ringing her phone today she decided to be kind.

Before Lisa could say "Hello" she heard "Lisa I miss you. Will you come see me?" Uri said excited. Yet, Lisa was still angry about his being with the other woman.

She responded to his request by saying, "Listen Uri, I'm busy, just as you are, so let's just keep it moving. You go your way and I will go mine."

There was silence and abruptly Uri said, "How would you like to fly to see me Friday evening here in Philadelphia for shopping Saturday and return home Sunday?" Lisa was so star struck by such a rich invitation, that she was speechless. Uri said, "Hello, are you still there?'

Then Lisa regained her composure and said, "Uri, what's this all about?"

Then he, becoming a bit irritated, said, "I know you should be treated well, so that's what I'm trying to do. I'm not perfect, but I am going to be leaving for a while, so I want to make you happy while I'm here. Is that fair?"

"Yes, that is very fair Uri and I would love to come visit you in Philly."

Chapter 15

Uri Makes Me Happy

"This car rental is just lovely" said Lisa.

"Yes, I thought we could run around Market Street and the malls for your shopping desires," said Uri with a smile, as Lisa smiled back at him.

"Shopping is one of my favorite activities, which reminds me, you are to be included," Lisa said happily.

"Oh, no" said Uri, "I am going to be in army gear for awhile."

Sunday evening as Uri and Lisa walked through their apartment doors with shopping bags and boxes; people were looking at them as if they had won the lottery. They smiled and continued on their way to Lisa's place first.

"Uri, I am so happy right now," said Lisa. "You bought me everything I wanted. How can I ever repay you darling?"

Uri laughed and said, "Come here you." She fell into his welcoming arms as he sat on her relaxing sofa. He embraced her with a satisfying kiss which lasted at least a couple of minutes. When they came up for air

Uri said, "Listen, my friend, all I want is that you will stay in contact with me by phone and mail to where I am deployed. Do you promise to do that?"

Lisa perked up after hearing his request that she could not refuse. "Oh Uri, it would be my pleasure to stay in contact with you. I will be honored." Lisa said as they kissed passionately again.

Tears ran down Lisa's face as she watched the black jeep drive out of the apartment complex parking lot for the last time. Uri had moved out and they had spent their nights together saying goodbye. Lisa could hardly believe this was happening. She felt so alone. What would she do without him? She began to cry frantically. Then her phone rang.

"Hello" said Lisa sounding upset. "This is why I knew to call you baby. You sound so upset. I want you to stop it and get yourself together and you relax! We have to both love our lives and encourage each other. Don't give up on yourself. I need you, I want you, and I'm coming back for you. Goodbye." Uri spoke to convince her.

Lisa gently hung up the phone as she began clearing up her emotional mannerisms. She knew he was right and she should listen to what he said but his leaving hurt her heart so much. The pain was powerful! Like nothing she had ever felt before.

"Oh, how could she go on?" she thought to herself. "But she must," her thoughts continued.

She laid across their familiar bed and fell asleep thinking of the times they shared together in her bed.

Chapter 16

Uri Breaks My Heart

Three months had passed and as Lisa was quickly going through her mail to see if a letter had arrived from Uri. The day finally came! It was in this batch of her mail. She was so nervous she could hardly open the envelope.

He talked of his work responsibilities, how hot the weather and how much he missed her. He planned to call as well but expected her to write as soon as possible. This scenario continued until he returned to the United States and located himself in Philadelphia. He was army captain now and planned to work as a civilian with his law degree that he acquired before he was deployed. He was happy and looking forward to seeing Lisa who was flying in from Upstate New York. She was so motivated to be in his loving arms once again.

They were at dinner at a very upscale restaurant when Uri looked Lisa in her eyes, giving her his full attention, took her by her right hand and said, "Lisa, you mean the world to me. You have been by my side and you have shown me your love over the years. Yet, my love, I have to move on," Lisa's mouth opened and her eyes widen as he continued, "I don't mean to hurt you but my life is changing and I have also" said Uri with sad expression on his face.

Lisa closed her mouth and checked her watch then said, "Take me to my hotel room and make me a flight for soon as possible for me to go home."

Uri said, "I understand how you must feel and I sincerely apologize. You don't deserve this but it can't be any other way. Please, understand me!"

Lisa stood up and hurried towards the restaurant door going towards his Mercedes in the parking lot. She was silent during the ride to the hotel. Uri went to her room and made her return flight arrangements for the next morning.

He continued to try to console her to no avail. Lisa was not anything except, "Just stop touching me!" She was so upset and starting to cry. She locked herself in the bathroom until he left.

Lisa turned the key as she opened her apartment door, after arriving home from Philly. She dropped her luggage on the floor and ran to her awaiting sofa and began to cry relentlessly. How could Uri treat her this way? She had expected so much more from their long time relationship.

"There must be another woman in his life," her mind beginning to ponder. "It's always another woman!", she pounded her pillow with that thought.

Then her mind went back to the conversation they had when he left to be deployed and he had told her to be "encouraged." Suddenly, she sat up, went to the bathroom, took a shower and lounged in her flowered robe while drinking a cup of green tea. She decided to do some cable channel surfing to relieve her mind of constant thoughts of what she had experienced.

As Lisa turned the tv channel she could hardly believe an episode of an old Billy Graham Christian Crusade program was showing. Lisa watched intensely and it began to give her uplift in her down spirit. She viewed the show until the program conclusion. Then she stood up, walked to her window, looking into the night sky and began to all of a sudden laugh. She laughed until she walked over and picked up her Bible off her coffee table. She thought the scripture that said, "My grace is sufficient for thee, my strength is made perfect in weakness. (2 Corth. 12:9)

This was the turning point of her entire evening. She began to realize that all along she had been putting her faith and hope in men. And they were always a disappointment to her in one way or another. Now Lisa knew what she had to do without hesitation.

The Storm
has Passed

Chapter 17

Jesus is the Man Forever

All week long Lisa was filled with anticipation about the coming Sunday. She had spoke with her friends Nia and Joy as they were accompanying her to the Sunday morning church service. Although they had gone to many church services before, this one was so very different for Lisa.

The tree ladies sat comfortably in the church pew and joined in with the service as usual. Then came the time for the Pastor giving the invitation to come to the Lord Jesus and give your life to him. Calmly Lisa stood up and walked to the front of the church. Today was the difference from all other Sunday services for the rest of her life.

Lisa had finally decided that Jesus was the "best man" that ever happened to her. She did not want to spend another moment out of his fellowship. She wanted Jesus as her personal Savior; she wanted to be a member of the church and planned to live her life sincerely for God our Father.

What a new beginning that Sunday service was for Lisa. Joy and Nia were already church members and supportive of Lisa's steps into her new walk with eternal life with Jesus Christ the Savior of the world. Lisa kept attending church weekly. She joined the church choir and sang faithfully for several years until she was asked to assist with the youth ministry which she joyfully accepted.

Lisa would talk to her dates on the phone and meet them out at restaurants. She decided that Jesus was the best unseen man that had ever happened to her and choose not to disappoint him with much sensual behavior. After enjoying her life with her new lifestyle, she decided to write a book. She accomplished this goal within 6 months and it was on the New York Times best sellers list, selling over a million copies. Lisa went to Los Angeles to study at screen writing school where her book was picked up and made into a movie. Lisa went on to live a very happy and hopeful.

Chapter 17b

The Surprise Retreat

A few years had gone into the future and it was 3:00am as Lisa was pacing her living room floor. She was alone and upset! "I've accomplished all these spiritual goals and have a great life but I'm still not happy!" She shouted in her thoughts and continued… "What will it take? What should I be doing to make my life better?" She threw the china glass she had been drinking wine with.

As Lisa collapsed into the expensive chair to cry some more…her phone rang. She let it ring and ring feeling it was probably bad news anyways at that hour. Then she fell asleep comfortably in the living room.

Suddenly there was a phone ring again awakening her around 7am. The persistent calls made her decide to answer her phone. "Hello" she said reluctantly.

"Oh, my God! Lisa is this you finally?" said Shelli, Lisa's old high school friend. "Lisa dear, I won a 3 day trip to a Christian Retreat in Arizona! I really want you to go with me. This will be a fabulous time for us to get ready for our future emotionally. Please say you will come."

"Well, hello to you as also Shelli," said Lisa a bit sarcastic. "Let me think…for sure I will come with you. It is just what I need in this time of my life. Thank you so much!" Lisa said happily.

As the taxi approached the splendor of the Retreat location, Lisa and Shelli gave each other a healthy handshake of sheer peace. They had arrived!

There were taxi cabs lined up in front with ladies of many nationalities and various dress styles. We hurried from our taxi to go inside and mingle. The girls were hopeful for the best to occur.

The next morning the loud sound of Christian praise music was blasting the hallways to wake us. Then we began to hear: "This is the day our Lord has made…let us rejoice and be glad in it! Each day of your life is a gift…that is why it is called "the present" when you adhere into daily life…"

The inspirational moments went on for about 15 minutes.

Lisa looked at their schedule and seen it was 30 minutes to get dressed. Then they headed to a gourmet breakfast buffet. The food was delicious and much of it was unusual.

"Okay Sisters, we are about to take a 3 hour power walk! We want your knees high, feet off the ground and a smile on your face. Enjoy this walk!" said the stern staff.

It was almost 10:00am when we arrived back at the lodge. We were directed to this plush room of uniquely designed furniture. Everyone found a seat and the speaker began talking about "Dreams. Everyone needs dreams or what can be described as thoughts or visions that occur during sleep or a goal that is wished during a daydream." She talked and talked and more talk. Then suddenly she said, "I would like each one of you to share your dream which you thought about but did not pursue and why?" We all looked at each other and laughed quietly as we took turns speaking. I was awesome!

Lunch time came and went. The pizza served was a buffet of so many styles. Yet, we were limited to 3 slices with ice water to drink. LoL

Next we were directed to another larger open red room to site on the floor. There were mats, small weights and a sound system.

For 2 motivating hours we did mediation..(deep thinking, light breathing, and no talking) The yoga was very relaxing. We did moves I would never expected but it was so much fun! Then we had music therapy...some Country, Blues, Jazz, and Christian songs which made us reflect, cry, and get so inspired to face the world!

It was now 3:00pm and we were given a pad and stamped envelope as we went back to our bedroom to rest and write a family member about our experience.

I heard a bell ringing and I went to the lobby to see why. There were several ladies dressed in white uniforms with towels across their arms. The staff girl began to say, "Ladies for the next 1.5 hours you can choose to have a pedicure, manicure or massage. Since you're here for 3 days choose a different choice each day. Thank You!"

"Well, now your cookin" said Shellie.

"I know...this as wonderful with a choice each day. I want all 3 because I enjoy them all," said Lisa.

It was dinner time before we knew it. We were enjoying ourselves so much with the spa that dinner could have waited. Yet, we were pushed to stay on schedule and found ourselves at a dinner with so much glass and class. We were told we were to practice "etiquette" for when we are eating out at fine restaurants or occasions. Such as, which fork goes with what plate, etc. OMG It was such an interesting time learning those rules.

Dinner was really fulfilling and as we headed to a large classroom designed like a college auditorium for our Bible Study Discussion group for 2 hours. I was feeling as if "tingling" was my middle name. I really felt fabulous! And now to learn about the Bible – what more could we ask for. Thanks Jesus!

"Ladies, Ladies...It is now relaxation time with the fire pit on the patio...Come along now. This is the last activity of the day." said the staff gentleman. As we walked outside onto the patio, it was absolutely sensational! There was beautiful seating areas, various types of food, flowers, soft instrumental music, bright candles, glorious smells and magazines. Shelli and I chose to roast marshmellows. We could hardly eat another bite! As I lay back on the patio seating, I began to think about my future aspirations and how hope was still alive!

The next 2 days was the same schedule with new information and food. Some days had little surprises like a Bingo game with prizes at one group session. Also, "Choosing and Waiting for the Right Man" at a group meeting, etc.

The 3 days were just stunning. I felt like a new person! The only thing they did not do was – makeovers with hair and make up. I guess because this was a Christian Retreat" Lisa laughed to Shelli.

As the two friends boarded the air plane to return home, they could hardly contain the zeal they had to share with others. The knowledge they had learned from their experience made them know they had hope for their future goals to be done and not just thought about in their minds.

$\mathscr{C}$hapter 18

"Success"

Lisa was becoming stronger and more beautiful in character. Her phone was ringing daily for speaking engagements, book signings and movie promotions since she relocated to her Pasadena, California condo.

For Lisa each day was a new and exciting experience on her journey. Meeting new people at luxury locations was really motivation for her stay focused with her appointments made by her personal assistant Diamond. She was exceedingly professional and dedicated to Lisa's goals.

Diamond was 25yrs and married to her wonderful high school sweetheart with no children. They were dedicated to their careers since her husband was a lawyer aged 35yrs and being very much in love while traveling yet being on call at a moment's notice.

Here is some of the information Lisa spoke at the Youth Event in Orlando, Florida to a group of teens. This knowledge she shared was very meaningful as she strived to make a positive impression on the youth attending.

As Lisa stood behind the curtain waiting for her name to be called for her introduction – she began to feel her blood pressure rise. What if they do not receive what I say? What if I click wrong on my tablet? What if they leave before I'm finished?

Suddenly, Lisa's attention was drawn to the sound of her name. The curtain opened and she began to walk towards the podium. The applause was thunderous! It sounded and felt so good to hear such a wonderful reception. Then it went to complete silence as I stood viewing the many young faces before me.

Lisa gave a warm smile while looking attentively into the large crowd. They responded by making a happy laugh at her.

She looked down at her tablet and began to speak, "How many of you would care to know about 'The Bi-Polar Survival Guide?'"

Lisa raised her head to register the reaction and it was quite motivating. Oh how thankful Lisa was that the youth were interested! Then she slowly but confidently began to speak aloud.

*C*hapter 19

"Bi-Polar Survival Guide"

"The Bi-Polar Survival Guide" as she took a sip of her tropical water and began to read with assurance:

Bi-Polar symptoms have extreme mood swings such as being all over the place in thought and actions. The person shows different personalities: sometimes happy and sometimes paranoia, other times feelings that people are against and want to hurt you, feelings that you are better dead for yourself and others and having the belief that no way would you be successful in life; just feeling hopeless.

What is the answer? You have to stay on your medication prescribed by your doctor. Yes, you will feel resentment towards taking the medication that keeps you balanced in your brain. You will ask yourself, 'Why should I have to take medication everyday for the rest of my life?

Yes, it will keep me stable and "normal" as other people are living daily.'

Now missing the medication will lead you to 'mania'. You will begin to feel a 'high'. It makes you feel very important and superior to others like you have 'power'. You are a human radar. People can see you through walls. You hear voices saying things that you should say or do. You start writing franticly to remember what is being said as you listen. The voices talk about you...saying things that are negative such as: 'There is no hope for her.'; 'There is no need for him.'; 'There is no way out.'

You hold your ears to try not to listen. You consider taking a trip with no luggage. You find yourself pacing the floor in circles and unable to relax or sleep while twisting your hands. Your mind is racing with thoughts of what to do next or tomorrow. You are very restless and feeling energized.

Then there is a trigger that causes you to fall into a deep depression. You do not want to do the things you usually do like cook, shower, shop, visit family or friends as well as to stop going to work or church.

The room you are laying in bed or on the sofa draws you and closes you inside yourself. You do not have the strength to get up. Now you're feeling anxiety and fear in many ways. Fear to eat - the food may be poisoned. Fear to sleep – maybe you will have nightmares or may not awake.

Otherwise, all you want to do is sleep day and night. The noise becomes 'messages' telling you some secret that only you can understand. When you watch television the shows are talking about you and your life – teaching and telling you some direction.

When family or friends notice the significant change in your behavior, you try to avoid them. You get away from their alerting you of your need for help. You do not want to believe or to trust what they have to say although, so deep inside, you are crying for help.

HELP - Being an Inpatient

Some people will allow a family member or friend to get them to a mental health facility or a hospital emergency room for help. This will allow a psychiatric evaluation of the person to observe what the condition of the patient and what is the best therapy.

Now for those who refuse to allow 'help', the police should be called and the person with the mental health issues will be removed from their location; put in the police car and escorted to the psychiatric facility or hospital to remain with the person until evaluated by the doctor as well as staff for them to be addressed.

If the person is found to be considered mentally unstable, there could be a mandatory admission for prescribed medication by psychiatrist with talk therapy as well as bed rest with meals for stabilization of the patient.

After the 72 hrs stay, the patient can be discharged to receive 'Outpatient Services' from an appointed Psychiatrist for medication and talk therapy (life skills) for support on a weekly or monthly basis by appointment.

Otherwise, if the patient is in need of extensive therapy form the mental health facility... daily appointments with psychiatrists, group discussion sessions, television for relaxation, meals and rooms as well as visitation from family. This occurs daily until the patient is prescribed their release into supportive care.

HELP - Being an Outpatient

This can be an up and down journey or smooth if the person decides. The key to a peaceful and successful transition to the "outside" or to be living in society is to:

Place all your medication in a store purchased "weekly pill box" labed day and night by sections. This will allow easy access when it is scheduled time to take your mecication.

Make your appointments with your doctor and have a purchased current "wall calendar" to write your appointments on the day and circle it to alert you when your appointments are scheduled.

Make a phone call to your doctor's office 2 days before your appointment to confirm your appointment is still scheduled.

Attend support groups if they are available for you. Their information and supportive encouragement are valuable for your well being for a good daily attitude.

If you work – please do not discuss your mental health issues at work! Do not think people are talking about you or want to hurt you when those thoughts come to your mind. Instead, have happy and caring attitude as well as be professional in your daily work habits.

If you are a stay at home parent or if you work from home or are disabled or retired – since you spend the majority of your time at home...do not allow yourself to become depressed or to feel lonely. Think about an activity that will give you positive self-esteem. Such as getting a part time job position, become a volunteer at an organization such as the Rescue Mission, Salvation Army, a hospital or join a church choir or take on painting or write a book.

Talk with someone on the phone or in person every day. Do not become a lone wolf. When you call about your bills or services, chat with the customer service representative. Call a family member or friend you have not spoken to in a while. Do not wait for them to call you. Also, consider taking a vocational class to learn a new skill and meet new people in the process.

Watch the television church ministries often and educate yourself about the wisdom of God. Developing yourself spiritually is a key growth and happiness. Have a paper and pen to write the scriptures and knowledge shared during each message or show. Also, give a donation and order the cd's and books offered to be able to listen at home or in your car to saturate yourself with the presence of God. Thank you for listening.

As Lisa finished her speech, she decided to answer a few questions and then was hurried away to her next engagement.

Chapter 20

My Radio Invitation

"Hello Ms L, you have been invited to speak in an interview on the black radio station this Saturday on its Community Forum hour. Isn't that great?" Diamond said on Lisa's voice mail.

Ms L kindly laid her iphone on her kitchen counter and began preparing her dinner. She thought about what she would talk about and then it came to her mind: Motherhood and Money are subjects that most people are interested in today.

"Good morning, Ms L. How are you this fine morning?" said Diamond as she walked in the room where Ms L was sitting at her desk.

Lisa did not respond but looked up at her personal assistant and replied, "What is the name of the DJ at the radio station who will interview me this Saturday?"

"Oh, his name is Skip. He is also sending a limo for you to arrive at the station on time", Diamond said laughing.

"So you find that funny?" said Lisa.

"Actually, I think it's rather cute and professional as well Ms L." said Diamond.

"Good afternoon ladies and gentlemen! So glad you could tune in with us today because we have a Special guest known as "Lisa". She is an author, artist, and speaker. A movie has been made about her book 'A Hopeful Single Life'. She is going to discuss 2 subjects with us today," Skip introduced. "Ms Lisa, how are you today?"

"Well, actually I'm excited to be here and I look forward to sharing my wisdom with you and the listening audience," said Lisa.

"Well, let's get started. What is your first subject to discuss Ms Lisa?" said Skip.

"My first subject is on 'Motherhood'. You see each hour, day, month and year should be a thoughtful action of love towards your child as an investment in their future. Each thought or action as directed towards your child should be beneficial for the good of the child. Each time you talk to your child it should be to teach, explain, give direction, protection, nurture or support your child with caring help. Each time you feed, clothe, shelter, travel, educate, motivate or inspire your child it should be to comfort them with appreciation." Lisa concluded.

"Great...now let's take some questions." said Skip "Caller number one, Mya, what is your question?"

"My question is: What should I do if I become pregnant before I planned to?"

"Like my mother told me – Make a list of all your appointments and keep them: medical and financial. Stay close to your friends and family for support. Also, pray to God all day long each day for help and thank him for his blessings."

"Now let's go to subject two for our listeners" said Skip the DJ.

"For sure" Lisa began. "Money is an expression of a person's wealth but it is as well your friend. It buys you goods and services. It pays people for their work. It is an investment for the future. Money should be enjoyed and appreciated! Care and respect should be shown towards it. It can be managed well to allow the comforts of life to be experienced and not only viewed. Money should be used to bring life into this world as well as prepare for the termination of life when it comes. Money is a benefit not an enemy. Care about money and it will care about you!"

"My My My, it's getting hot in here Lisa. Let's take our next caller with a financial question. Is this Steve?"

"Yes, Lisa, my question is: What is a budget?"

"Mr. Steve, wonderful question! A budget is the accurate plan for using money. First, you list all your income sources and add them for total. Then you list all your expenses or bills and add them. Then you subtract the expenses total from the income total. And you juggle to make it balance." Lisa said in closing the conversation.

"Well, Lisa, you certainly gave us some wisdom today! Thank you so much." Skip said ending the segment.

Skip gave Lisa a hug and said he would certainly like her to return soon. Lisa was so pleased that he was satisfied as she, Diamond and Ralph, her often paid personal assistant who accompanied them on engagements that required security, stepped into the limo.

Chapter 21

I Miss Mom

Lisa fell on her bed thinking about her mother. She spoke with her Mom on the phone weekly but she was missing her in the heart. She began to dial her mother's number and heard, "Hello who is calling?" the voice said.

"Mother, I want to come visit you in two weeks." said Lisa.

"Come when you like Honey; I will be here. The Lord has not called me home yet" she said with a chuckle.

"Mom, I really miss you and your good cooking" the daughter said.

"Child, I do not cook like I use to but you could help me cook something good." said Mother Beckie.

"Great, Mom! That is all I wanted to hear. I will see you in two weeks and I will call you this Sunday. Goodbye for now." said Lisa.

"Goodbye child" said Mother.

∞

"You lovely ladies can be seated here and your waiter will be with you shortly" said the attendant.

Mother Beckie and Lisa sat comfortably in the luxury restaurant that Lisa surprised her mother with after church service. "You know Mom when the Pastor preached that God cannot build you up until he tears you down. I can totally relate since my ruined marriage made me feel hopeless. Yet, when I wrote my book and my life revived with so much joy as well as excitement! I absolutely agree with his point of view" Lisa said confidently.

"Yes, sweetheart. I am so pleased you regained your strength and purpose. I was so worried about you during your struggles and I kept you in my prayers" said the Mother.

"Yes, Mom I prayed, attended church, watched TV ministries, read my Bible, was a giver often, and just believed in Jesus to help me as I worked at making my life better" said Lisa.

"Oh yes darling, you need to look at your art while you are home. It is still very inspiring to see your talent. Although, you did not finish college for it, at least you did get your Business Administration degree. Of which, I am sure is helping you now," said Mother.

"Oh Mom you are so right! As is written, All things work together for good to them who are called according to his purpose." said Lisa.

"Okay Lisa there you go preaching. Add this to your list of abilities" the Mother said happily.

"Well, here comes our waiter so let us get ready for dinner. It feels wonderful to chat with you, Mom," as Lisa reached over to give her a kind and loving hug.

(Knock, Knock) (Knock, Knock)

"Mom, who is at the door?" said Lisa. Mother Beckie walked to the door to see who was there knocking. Well to her surprise it was Octavia, Lisa's high school friend.

"Goodmorning Mother Beckie! I heard Lisa is home; is she here?" said Octavia.

"Yes, Octavia, she is here but not up yet" said the Mother.

Then Lisa spoke up and yelled, "Octavia, come on up girl." In a flash Octavia was sitting before Lisa happy as she could be! The girls talked about their past experiences and laughed so much.

Mother Beckie yelled to the girls, "Don't forget to look at your art Lisa" she yelled,

"Alright already, Mom. We are going to the guest bedroom now to look in the closet for my art." Lisa said hurriedly.

The art was so excellent and should be viewed by many. "Your art is so interesting. Do you plan to expose more use of it" said Octavia.

"Actually, I have had it in exhibits and come close to selling them. Yet, they are my babies and I may sell prints of them in the future." said Lisa.

When Lisa was preparing to leave her Mother's home, tears were shed with their hugs. Lisa promised to return sooner rather than later.

Chapter 22

The Unique Talk Show

It was five AM and Lisa entered the office building filled with excitement. This was her first talk show appearance in weeks. She knew the best had to come or her reputation would be ruined. So many people were running around handling their business. The glam squad began their work on Lisa with her hairstylist, makeup artist, wardrobe, etc. Lisa felt so important!

Suddenly the host of the talk show entered the area and Lisa felt her presence. She walked over to Lisa and held her right hand calmly and said, "You will be great...Just relax while being yourself. You can do that right?" Lisa smiled with assurance and replied," I've never felt better and I'm excited to be on your so popular show. Thank you again for inviting me. Just try not to challenge me very much please!" They laughed and began to walk towards the show set to be seated in a very plush setting.

The host began saying, "Lisa, would you share with us what your perspective of "Power" is in today's society?"

"Sure I would love to share my opinion on 'Power' said Lisa. She stood and walked directly over to the glass podium while looking at the audience as well as the television cameras. She began to speak slowly and a bit nervous.

"Ladies and gentlemen true Power begins with Prayer because prayer is the action of speaking to God especially to give thanks or ask for something which is the hope or wish for many on a daily basis. It can be voiced out loud with people or quietly in your thoughts. To pray is something a person feels he or she ought to do because it is morally right. Since morals are concerned with or relating to what is right and wrong in human behavior...prayer is powerful when done from the heart with focus on certain subjects areas." Lisa said pausing.

"Next you beautiful people, we all should seek Peace because peace is the freedom from public disturbance or war allowing a quiet and calm state of mind which is in harmony among people which is the desire of most men and women. Peace comes in many forms. It should be enjoyed and appreciated. You can reach for peace by being careful of your words and actions to follow after that which is good. Peace is powerful especially when love is allowed to be the motive or direction of the people." said Lisa glancing at the audience.

She paused a moment to sip from her glass of water. She coughed softly and resumed speaking. "Next my intelligent people is Prosperity which actual prosperity is the state of being successful usually be making money allowing strong and healthy growth in life which is the dream of many people. Most believe that excessive cash is the goal of working or investing to gain wealth; the lottery, Casinos, stocks, bonds, life insurance, etc. all come into play as a means to an end for riches also. Yet, true wealth is not the accumulation of money but is love. To be able to love God, with all your mind, heart, and soul and to love your neighbor is the key." Lisa said happily.

"Finally my precious believers is Praise... to glorify God as expression of approval in worship is usually done at church. Yet, to offer thanks to God for his goodness and blessings can be done at anytime and anywhere. God is available to hear our praise 24 hours a day. When we express our appreciation to God by singing, giving, helping others and talking about his ways, we open the windows of heaven for the joy of the Lord which is our strength. Yes, to praise our God daily in good and bad times allows the door of the power of God to be opened and released into our lives in ways of blessings expected and unexpected." Lisa paused.

"Now all this I shared with you today is to influence your thinking to proper thoughts which have "Power". Please continually feed your mind with intelligence and truth. Thank you!" Lisa bowed her head slightly and walked over to be seated.

The audience gave a loud applause and the host said congratulations her on a job well done. As Lisa was leaving the studio to enter her limo, she looked and viewed a very shinny object on her pathway.

The object was so brilliant that Lisa reached for it to retrieve it. Suddenly, upon her touching the object... Lisa was transformed into the dimension where she heard the great voices of much people in heaven saying, "Alleluia; salvation and glory and honor and power, unto the Lord our God.

For true and righteous are his judgments: for the hath judged the great whore, which did corrupt the earth with her fornication, and hath avenged the blood of these servants in her hand. And again they said, "Alleluia!" And her smoke rose up forever and forever.

And the four and twenty elders and four beasts fell down and worshipped God the sat on the throne saying, "Amen; Alleluia!"

And a voice came out of the throne saying, "Praise our God, all ye his servants, and ye that fear him, both small and great." Lisa's vision heard more as it were the voice of a great multitude, and as the voice of many waters, and as the voice of mighty thundering saying, "Alleluia: for the Lord God omnipotent reigneth. Let us be glad and rejoice, and give honour to him: for the marriage of the Lamb is come, and his wife hath made herself ready. And to her was granted that she should be arrayed in fine linen, clean and white: for the linen is the righteousness of saints. And the vision said unto Lisa, "Write, Blessed are they which are called unto the marriage supper of the Lamb" And he saith unto me, "These are the true sayings of God." (Revelation 19:1-9)

Chapter 23

My Hospital Trip

As he was cupping my left shoulders with his left arm and holding my right hand looking down into my face saying with so much worry, "Are you alright? Lady, Lady are you alright?"

As my eyes came into focus of this world I smiled a bit as I noticed the large crowd of people starring at me with so much concern. He spoke again to me directly in my eyes saying, "Don't worry; an ambulance is on the way here any minute. Just relax dear!"

I was so amazed at his "take charge" and really comforting male individual attitude. Especially, since Diamond and my security guard were kneeling next to me crying.

The ambulance arrived all of a sudden and transferred me to the nearest hospital east of the city. Diamond was with me making phone calls to everyone who needed to know about me. After all the medical procedures were completed and I was given the all clear to go home. I simply had passed out from dehydration...so THEY say.

It felt so comfortable to head towards the hospital door to the exit. When a surprise occurred: "Take Charge Gentleman" was approaching me with a bouquet of flowers. I could hardly believe what was happening!

"Hello, Miss Lisa. How are you now? You had me so worried. What was wrong with you after your stellar performance on the Talk Show?" he said.

I explained to him the doctors conclusion and that I was on my way home.

He said, "Well, I have a very important appointment. May I have your phone number to call and check on you later?"

I am a Life Coach and I am meeting with my client over dinner. 'Well, Oh Happy Days' I thought in my mind. "Sure," I gave him my phone number and felt so excited about it! Especially since it had been awhile since she had been dating due to her busy schedule and lack of male contacts.

Chapter 24

My Life Coach

So once I was showered and relaxing in my own bed the phone started ringing. Diamond was diverting the calls because I was not to be having conversations at that time. The next day the phone rang at 6am and I was so tempted to answer since Diamond had gone home. Guess who it was? Yes, it was "Mr. Gentleman".

"Are you awake, my Lady?" he asked with a happy attitude.

"Well, I guess now" said Lisa softly. "I have not awakened this early since I was at a retreat I attended a while ago."

"Oh, that is fantastic that you have attended a retreat. You really have to inform me of your experience and benefits one day" he said.

Lisa was hesitant for a few minutes then calmly said, "It would be wonderful if you told me your name." as she laughed.

He said, "Actually, I want to keep you in suspense a little longer. I want you to get to know me rather than judge me by name."

Lisa was so shocked, she was speechless.

Remember, he was a Life Coach, so he began to have sessions with Lisa in exchange for her cooking them dinner. They had a brother and sister type relationship: no hugging, no kissing, and no sex. This went on for about a month. Then one evening he decided to tell her two subjects after the kitchen was cleaned up.

"Lisa, my name is Lester. I did not want to tell because people in school would call me "Luster". I am rather embarrassed of my name as he lowered his head.

"Oh my goodness"' said Lisa, "I think it is appealing. You certainly will not forget it" she smiled.

"Ok, great! Well then, the next subject on my agenda this evening is this: I think you are the strongest, most intelligent and certainly beautiful client as well as friend to me. Therefore, I would like to reward you with a trip…yes trip…you and I". He pause and did a drum roll on the kitchen counter, "to Las Vegas in two weeks for the weekend." Lester said cautiously.

"Are you kidding me?" said Lisa, "I have always wanted to visit there. Oh my God! Jesus you are so good to me! Lester, thank you so much for your thoughtfulness," as she gave him a hug but no kiss.

"Okay, we will talk more tomorrow…have a good night," as he walked out of Lisa's door.

Chapter 25

The Las Vegas Arrival

Lisa was tossing and turning not able to sleep. She was so elated about her trip. Just a Vegas trip with a wonderful friend and all expenses paid. It was definitely a dream come true. No, it was a miracle!

Ring! Ring! "Hello" said Lisa.

"Are you ready to go to the Casino in the hotel before we visit the pool area and later go to the Event.? Lester said.

"Oh, absolutely Lester. I am more than ready. I am on my way to your door, bye" said Lisa in a hurry.

The Casino was filled with so many people. The colorful slot machines made you eager to give them a try with your money. The beautiful girls dancing on top of the tables. The card tables with men and women trying their luck. Okay, I'm ready for the pool!

There were so many sexy and exciting guys and girls playing in the water, sitting on the pool sides and drinking from the bar. We sat on the sofa area and relaxed like you would not believe…it was sunset and such a unreal atmosphere. Am I really here? Yes, I am! Oh, yes I am!

As the time went on we started walking towards the Event location. People were everywhere. So many designs and shinning bright lights with all colors in the night. Yes, this is Vegas!

The next morning at breakfast Lester took me by my hand and looked me in my eyes and said, "Lisa, I had another reason for your coming here with me." Lisa's eyes peerked up as she listened attentively to Lester.

"Lisa, we get along so well. God, I really enjoy and value your company. So, I would like to ask you... he stopped to breathe deeply then continued, "Lisa, I would like us to go into business together. I want us to go into Real Estate. We buy some properties and lease them to an agency that cares for people with disabilities or veterans. We have the money...let's invest in our future!

Lisa's heart sank and she almost fell on the floor. How could he not ask her to marry him? It was such a set up! Yet, she caught herself. They were companions. Marriage was not in the cards for them. They were not even romantic to each other.

After a long quiet period, Lisa re-grouped and said, "Lester that would be a great idea! I would like to go to real estate school to learn the basics. We really should prepare for our future. So many people are successful in real estate I have heard. Let's go for it!"

"Yes, Lisa...I'm so glad you are on board with the idea. You are really the best!" said Lester as he was getting into his black Seville car.

Chapter 26

Nowhere- Somewhere Fast

Lester and Lisa returned to their home city elated! They attended a notable real estate school, bought and leased several properties as they shared a successful partnership for about 2 years.

Lester met a man on a business trip which lead him to realize he was actually gay. They began dating long distance for a few months. They later married and he moved in with Lester.

Lisa was so bewildered and lonely for the way things use to be between them. After Lester's marriage they communicated now on a business level.

So Lisa was advised by Lester to adopt a foster child. She would be making a contribution to society as well as her own well being. She patiently discussed it with her family and friends. They all agreed it could be fulfilling.

After a long time of procedures, Lisa did qualify to adopt a brother and sister pre-teens. They moved into a comfortable home as Christians living compelling lives working towards the days to come.

Printed in the United States
By Bookmasters